LESSONS

JOEL OPPENHEIMER

LESSONS

SELECTED POEMS

EDITED BY DENNIS MALONEY
INTRODUCTION BY DAVID LANDREY

WHITE PINE PRESS / BUFFALO, NEW YORK

White Pine Press
P.O. Box 236
Buffalo, New York 14201

www.whitepine.org

Acknowledgments appear on page 245.

Thank you to the family and estate of Joel Oppenheimer for their
assistance and cooperation.

Publication of this book was made possible, in part, by public funds
from the New York State Council on the Arts with the support of
Governor Andrew M. Cuomo and the New York State Legislature,
a State Agency; and with funds from the National Endowment for
the Arts, which believes that a great nation deserves great art.

Printed and bound in the United States of America.

Cover image: "Walking in the Shade" by Melissa Lofton. Used by
permission of the artist. www.mlofton.com

ISBN 978-1-945680-00-7

Library of Congress number 2016949215

LESSONS

Contents

from *The Woman Poems*

from *Names, Dates and Places*

from *At Fifty: A Poem*

from *Generations*

from *New Spaces*

INTRODUCTION

DAVID LANDREY

Writing about Andrew Marvell's poem, "The Garden," William Empson spoke of Marvell's achievement of "The Ideal Simplicity Approached by Resolving Contradictions." Joel Oppenheimer (1930–1988) [hereafter simply "Joel," as he was to all who knew and loved him] achieved an elegant simplicity. Simplicity was not, for Joel, opposite to complexity; he was keenly aware of complexity, that it was greater in our time, and he faced it boldly, knowing well that avoidance was doomed to fail. The opposite of simplicity (and damning to it) was expressed by Emerson in *Nature* as follows:

> When simplicity of character and the sovereignty of ideas is broken up by the prevalence of secondary desires,—the desire of riches, of pleasure, of power, and of praise,—and duplicity and falsehood take place of simplicity and truth, the power over nature as an interpreter of the will is in a degree lost; new imagery ceases to be created, and old words are perverted to stand for things which are not; a paper currency is employed, when there is no bullion in the vaults.

Oh how Joel despised "duplicity," finding it all around him, especially in the world of politics. "Old words ... perverted to stand for things which are not": battling this perversion was central to everything Joel said and wrote, and the battle was revealed in the presence of many polarities and the resolution thereof—"polarities" rather than "contradictions."

Major shifts characterized Joel's life: from his Yonkers upbringing to Black Mountain College (by way of failures at the University of Chicago and Cornell); from Black Mountain to Greenwich Village; from the Village out to what he called New Spaces; from instability to a final settling in Henniker, New Hampshire, happily wed to "the beautiful Theresa" Maier[1, 2] As this progression occurred, as he dealt with the insecurities involved, he resolved his polarities, leaving a legacy of profound love.

I knew Joel in his New Spaces, a different Joel from what others knew. He had lived through two failed marriages, and although I came to know his children, I did not experience his anxiety about earlier times except through his poetry and in later conversation. I did not know him during his struggles with alcohol; he dried out in 1970, and we met in 1978. I was teaching a course in Black Mountain poets at Buffalo State College when two students said that they wanted to meet him, so we three set out, along with a deaf white cat, to visit him at his flat in Westbeth. We did not call in advance, strangely enough, but called from a phone booth in the Village. His affectionate welcome speaks volumes about the openness of his spirit.

*****

The overarching polarity of Joel's life and writing, then, involved geography. His life in Greenwich Village was confined to a few blocks, wherein he had rituals, repeated regularly, presumably as a kind of control, a hedge against chaos. He ate at the same greasy spoon, drank at the same bars (most notably, the Lion's Head), and played war games constantly (paradoxical for this man of peace). He also wrote "occasional poems," what those who knew him early understood as his primary mode: wedding poems, birthday poems, holiday poems, and, especially, poems for Groundhog Day, loved by him as the time when Persephone returned from the dead to bring Spring. The Village was his ground of being and provided the daily material for his work.

In 1970, Joel became a columnist for *The Village Voice*. In the Prefatory Note to *On Occasion* (1973), the last of his primarily occasional poems, he wrote:

> goethe says somewhere that occasional poetry is the highest form of art; when it succeeds i incline to agree with him—by success i mean when the poem moves past the

personal impetus for writing it but preserves the solid air of that impetus; in other words, that the poem, hopefully, may be meaningful far beyond the immediate situation.

He had always, to some degree, moved past the personal, but he would do so on a much larger scale in the remaining years of his too-short life.

The *Voice* columns bridged the gap between old life and new. They permitted him to rant, thus liberating his poetry for a grander scale. He could develop his discursive voice to the fullest, freeing him in his poetry to work outside of what his master, Charles Olson, called logic and classification, to plunge into the middle (or, as he liked to say, the muddle) of a field. At Black Mountain, Joel studied with Olson and would attempt to write Olsonesque poems, causing the master to write on his manuscript, "Dear Joel, I have enough trouble writing these damn things myself. Find your own voice." When Olson visited New York a few years later (probably 1961), Joel shyly asked him to read "The Fourth Ark Royal" (p. 34 in this volume). Olson commented, "Great. This is what I've been waiting for. You've always had this discursive quality, like you tell great jokes, and you've made it happen in the poems."[3] But as the *Voice* columns developed, Joel realized that the discursive voice became "awfully pretentious and sententious" in the poems, that it needed to be modified. In his Charles Olson Memorial Lectures (1982), he said, "I had to get out of [discursiveness] through the *Voice* columns and get back to the sparseness. Retain the voice but stop throwing so much stuff in."

Joel spoke of *The Woman Poems* as the last manifestation of the old voice. Perhaps, but already we see in them (note, especially, "Screaming Poem" p. 83) the new sparseness. He always said that these poems were a rare instance of his having been "given" the material, "that the muse had come in and was sitting there." Two years before *The Woman Poems* came bubbling forth, he had heard Robert Bly lecture about the Great Mother, and, in 1973, he read Bly's "I Came Out of the Mother Naked." His old and new voices blended with Bly's material to produce this extraordinary work, one in which he courageously presented his habitual view of women—a classically male chauvinist view (although several women who were at Black Mountain found him frank in his sexuality but not objectionable)—and reexamined that view. In October 1978, he lectured to a class at Buffalo State College about *The Woman Poems*. Although one woman took the book back to the college store and demanded her money back, the women in the class eventually understood what he had accomplished, that he acknowledged his (and the dominant male society's) proclivities and even, as in "Screaming Poem,"(page 83) confronted the woman within himself. The men were slower to understand.[4]

The breakthrough in his poetry produced a breakthrough in his sense of place and in his vision. Later in the year of *The Woman Poems*, Joel wrote "Poem for the New Year: 31 december 1973" (p. 117), in which, in dreams, he is being assaulted, first by Medusa:

> and i am saved
> by the old poet, he helps me
> break loose. he tells me
> he's never yet seen one would
> hold on if you fought long enough

and then by:

> a basilisk in my
> dream who also tried to freeze me.
> i woke abruptly, thrashing, safe
> again, as he scuttled across the floor.
> the basilisk does not grow
> older, does not ever change.

we walk on, and sleep each night.
he said: hold on, hold on,
until the new vision comes.
it comes, it opens up,
it always comes.

Charles Olson is the "old poet" mentioned in the poem (he died in 1970; a memory of him became the subject of Joel's second *Village Voice* column) as well as he who tells him to hold on.

Consider this polarity: that he needs to hold on, as in his Village rituals, yet a new, liberating vision is coming. The New Vision would go beyond geography (as increasingly he visited what he came to call his New Spaces) to myth, as it already had in *The Woman Poems* and as it would appear again and again in such poems as "Lessons, 1 & 2" (p. 158). He would find his own mythologies in both old and new places (consider, e.g., "A Village Poem" [p. 152], "Acts" [p. 164], "Cacti" [p. 177], and "Houses" [p. 191]).

In his new "geography" he has new takes on various polarities: on Stability and Change, on Inner Life and the Greater World, on Past and Future, on Male and Female, and—especially—on Order and Disorder. Most illustrative of where he finally arrived is the first poem of his last volume, "chaos" Although it appears on p. 217, I'll present it here:

chaos is where
we come from

form we reach
occasionally
then fall back
into chaos
to start again
renewed

inchoate
means beginning

comes from the root
to harness

getting into harness
is just the beginning

how we plow and
what we plant
determines the field

the field
determines
what feeds us
while we wait
to fall back
to grow again

About this, Rich Blevins said:

> I believe that Joel's working concept of chaos—that is, the process of art from disorder, and not the mistaken dichotomy that would hold art versus disorder—was conditioned and absorbed from Olson's understanding of Chaos, and his argument that postmodern poetics should be freed from the restrictions of logical systems and returned to the openness of the Homer-Hesiod imagination.[5]

Joel has packed the Hesiodic imagination into a small space but with maximum comprehension, a perfect blend of his discursive voice and a new sparseness. The "field" of this poem is in/is New Hampshire, the scene of the end of his life, a world where he became thoroughly comfortable, as if finally he could locate the ground beneath The Village. The act of planting by this poet well known for his erotic poetry is a final comprehension of the full nature of creative force. He arrived at an Ideal Simplicity, a fact additionally illustrated by his finally achieving his dream of creating a poetic line that succeeded without punctuation.

Finally, a comment on two seminal poems, "Time Out," (not included in this volume) written in my attic after a conversation with my wife, Kathy, about the perils of the Aswan Dam, and "Celebrating the Peace" (page 123). In "Time Out," Joel links his personal anguish to the duplicity of world leaders. "Celebrating the Peace" could have been a mere rant, but, in the keenness of his perception we are left, instead, with the blending of two voices, journalistic observation with religious chant. In the end, the blend produces a solitary, saddened, tragic cry. He truly believed in the validity of "the long, drawn-out losing fight."

*****

A brief comment on Joel's use of lower case. He variously attributed this to e.e. cummings, to Don Marquis, and to a broken shift key. He also said that he did not want to privilege any words by means of upper case.

I Joel's evolution is presented brilliantly by Lyman Gilmore's biography, *Don't Touch the Poet: The Life and Times of Joel Oppenheimer*, Jersey City, New Jersey: Talisman

House, 1998.

2 I read at Joel's and Theresa's wedding on November 4, 1984 in Rochester, New York, where he spent the 1984–85 academic year occupying the Gannett Chair in Language and Literature at Rochester Institute of Technology. This position, in Theresa's words, "meant that he had arrived, that he had a podium, that people cared to listen to him." (Quoted in the Gilmore biography.)

3 see Christopher Beach's "Interview with Joel Oppenheimer" in *Sagetrieb* 7:2, Fall 1988.

4 for this lecture and two others, see *Poetry, the Ecology of the Soul,* Buffalo, NY: White Pine Press, 1983, ed. by Dennis Maloney and David Landrey. This volume also contained a much shorter "Selected Poems."

5 from "From the Muddle Out: Chaos Theory and Some Poems by Joel Oppenheimer," delivered as a lecture at New England College and printed in *Talisman* #20, Winter 1999/2000 along with talks by Don W. Melander, Robert Bertholf, Edward Foster, David Landrey, Patrick Meanor, and M. G. Stephens.

LESSONS

NAMES AND LOCAL HABITATIONS:
SELECTED EARLY POEMS
1951–1972

The Dancer

for Katherine Litz

for Katy
    stands rooted, herself
to one spot
        becomes:
            the only spot we know.

Grows, in this spot, among:
                flowers
                love
                whatever's
her particular
        as we too
have particulars
        but she
flies free
        pulling.

Delight, unvarying
        Katy dances;
her dance's conjure:
        flowers;
her legs are suns to light
the seeds around, while
                on the wooden floor
her feet
know mud, know snow, know
spring

An Answer

what mercy is not
strained, what justice
not bought, what
love not used come thru.
my lady asks me
not without reason
where is pleasure in it. where sense.
my ear is not worth much
in these matters, tho it be
shellike, and acute.
offer beyond a dedication?
and a particular care.

The Bus Trip

images of J————————assail him.
the moon used to, but the moon is
an illuminated clock, he feels.
it doesn't particularly remind him or instruct.
when he rides on the bus with
drawings, a bag of apples, his
wife and lovely child, is he any
less or more the, a, fool.
if his child were not beautiful
what could he do and live. if his wife
were not beautiful what could he do and live.
these things are insanely important
to him. tho he lose his power facing them.
a woman, girl, across from him is
more beautiful than the world. he is
repelled. and pulls back. death.
the death of beauty, when it is beautiful, he
finds her. and dead. across from him
in a bus. the old man beside her. they
talk in Italian.
        a heavy sigh escapes him
when he goes. away from that across from him.
descends into the street. sketches, apples,
child, helps his pregnant wife. she
smiles. the child runs down
the street. images of J————
assail him. constantly. what shall he do.

The Bath

he will insist on
reading things into her simplest act.
her bath, which she takes
because he wills it so. her bath
she takes to cleanse herself.
ritual. ritual always
in his life. she takes her bath
to ready herself.
and himself more often than not decides
she wants him unbathed. manlike.
what his is most pleased about is
her continuing bathing.
in his tub. in his water. wife.

Provence

today i bathed my feet, like
some irish maiden hoping
for a lover
                —she would have to be
long-haired; i trust only long-haired women

and it is summer here, and still
men are talking about
another land, which had been
impossibly green and fruitful

yet i might have done
better, there, myself. i

might have written good songs, if
she had been faithful, and better, if
she were not, and also, polemic
against the betrayer, political,
tearing him down; with a choice
of rhetoric—between
rapier and the two-bitted
woods-axe, which i seem to favor,
being the man i am, using it
file-sharpened, to a good edge

well, as it is, either
silence, or silence and
action either way most brutal is
expected; and i would prefer a
milieu demanding hard work
—and fitting words to a tune

'fair night,
early rising,
the sun up,
the mist still rising, and
in the woods, sounds of small animals

       it is a hard travelling, toward you, with
       a hidden road

       it is hard to tell what
       i am complaining about

       wanting to know, i guess,
       that it is not even this for you

       which, whether or not it is a fine thing to be
       saying, especially at this point, still

'remember this hand
which touched you

'be ready upon the white palfrey, the
small and strong one, with
spirit; three
days from now,
at dawn.'

The Gardener

on the left branch, a
blossom. on the
top branch, a blossom.
which child is this.
which flowering
of me. which
gold white bloom.
which the force of my life.

Cartography

the ceiling of his bedroom
cracks into map shapes.
an island. harbors sunk in the island's perimeter.
two great rivers. a lake at the confluence.
while on the phone he draws plans of houses abstractedly,
or replots the defense of gettysburg.
on the bedroom wall, in detail, san francisco bay,
the hills marked and notated with the addresses of friends.
on the walls of the john,
hand-drawn and accurately scaled,
the devil's den and the round tops.
the lines outside vicksburg, petersburg, the wilderness
mile by mile engraved in his mind. carried with him
white oaks, where his great-grandfather fell.
he does not even know if this fact, this death,
exists for him outside of white oaks.
shall he not die also when he has no direction
before him, no plan of action, no campaign.
does he not find it impossible to move without
at least compass, or sun, gunter's chain, or a
measured pace, or the regular plat of a city's streets.
at one time his pace was exactly three feet.
with it he could determine miles, within a few yards.
or put it this way. if in his own islands
he could move freely. if he could take himself and his worlds.
build a continent of them, that might break him free.
if his children were more than milestones to him.
or if his wife more than the tracings of his finger
outlined before him. that might break him free.
but he will find it necessary to move himself.
this is the first action.

An Undefined Tenderness

an undefined tenderness came
into the relationship. we were
afraid of such things, still, it
became necessary, and we learned
not to put it down—or put it
this way, time and a senseless
friction wore a smooth edge.
finally, I think, we could face to it:
there is no love possible beyond
those first moments of fire and
trembling passion. this makes more
sense than a roomful of roses,
your ass, and my heart. and, desire
burns fiercely in me yet, i
ought to be satisfied.

The Fourth Ark Royal

for e. d.

time is an old lady
like madame defarge

she sits weaving us
into it, humming old
tunes, tunes we half
remember, or somehow
haven't heard at all
we say: gee, what are
the words to that, or,
what's the name, damn
it, or, how does the
rest of that go

we say what we can, is
the simple truth of it,
as if there were
simple truth wherever
time that old lady
enters in. she will
not be true to you,
and she will not be
true to me, she is an
old lady concerned with
the pattern she is
weaving, only every
stitch is true, and
might even have saved
nine

so we come, finally,
to a bar. there are
old friends, the women
are beautiful, someone
has money, the drinks
flow and flow, we talk,
in the end, that almost
comes to be the best for
us, that we talk, what
else were we constructed
for, even?

in the quiet
light of early spring one
comes on strange things in
bars, the other night it
was those young sailors
from the ark royal, the
fourth, i had to discover
by asking, talk again.
they thought the
first fought with
drake against the armada, the
second was in line with
nelson at trafalgar, the
third went down in the
north atlantic. now
the fourth sits at anchor
in new york bay, and
the young english sailors
flood ashore, they are

all over the city, even
in the cedars, asking:
is that a beatnik, and for
once honestly asked, they
ask as simply as if the
question were:

       what time
is it? or what is the
name of that tune? they
are here tonight, too, in this
bar where old friends are
meeting; helene said:
every time i look up there
is someone else i haven't
seen in eight years. what
is the name of that tune?
then we come to where we
have nothing more to
offer other than our bare
souls, and the old lady
giggles as she knits, she
thinks she has us there
but this is what we have
to come to, i keep telling
myself; what else to offer
an old friend, no gift,
not money, sex, liquor, not
an old suit, my cousin
eddie does that for me,
not even the graciousness of

our presence, christ, might
as well have a dinner
party for that. half
remembered what we have said
in the past beats as
firmly against us as the
pulse in this night's bourbon.

i thank you for it, that
a memory beats again as
solidly as you walking to
the platform, your feet
set solidly (your feet
set solidly in a different
way, of course than
mine) i saw the pace and
thought what tune is
that? what are the
words to it? and how
does the rest of it go?

we have beat the old
lady, and that's the
loveliness of it, sometimes
you do, even if she
doesn't know it, keeps on
knitting, weaving in four
ark royals, young
english sailors, your
kids, my kids, tunes we
ought to have remembered,

tunes that never did
exist, tunes that shouldn't
have existed, too many
drinks, and some drinks
that were perfect for
their time, our friends
gather round, we even
bowled a game, the perfections
of a grace directed at
the limited world a game is.

what tune is that?
how do the words go?
what's the rest of that tune?
this i want to give you
to take with you, send
me answers whenever you
get them, i'll tell bob
too, and charles and max,
whoever in this world of
ours might be listening,
one of us may find out,
if not, we haven't lost
anything...as if there
were anything to lose we
haven't already come onto
and made a decision about.

i'm sorry three ark royals
had to go down, planes from
the third crippled the

bismarck as she dashed from
the denmark strait trying
for france.

and even
this has no bearing, until
we give it one, whatever
it deserves. my friend,
i offer you a drink, my
bare soul, and a half
memory of when we last met.

and i remember best that
time is an old lady, like
madame defarge, somehow
weaving us all in, humming
old tunes we might not
remember, at the door.

N. B.

love is not memory, love
is the present act

is what have we done for
us lately, is where
am i, or you

you are sitting on a
rock in the moonlight
your red-blond hair
loose in the moonlight
you are crying

that was a long time
ago. a lot happened.

and if her hair sitting
before me is the same
shade, rarely found.

        your hair
is not love, love is
the present act.

New Blues for the Moon

for d. d.

i know your door
better than i know my own.

and ought to warn you
i bring habits into
every house. dirty
laundry here, supper
there, a quart or two
of beer, wine, whiskey.

the habits a man is
constructed of, ought
to know himself by thirty
if there's any good to him.

to you. and still haven't
figured out how a woman
walks. my last duchess
had small hard nates. this
is a different matter.

infinite variety in a
grain of laudanum.
infinite variety in
by god what are you doing now.

i know your door better
than i know my own.

Flora

for j. g.

wandering jew even
your one purple
blossom gone, now
only the green and
purple leaves aglow
in the evening

you keep on growing
yet she swears every
other plant died for her

once every sabbath or so
the purple flower reappears,
now on this branch, now
down there on that one

the simple and insensate
act we all live by, one
purple flower
         you are
composed of all the green
leaves you could dream of

ach, i make too much of you

A Prayer

oh, the word, and the
bloody wine that
changes it. the
bloody wine that is
my body. the word.
the wine, the body.
they move in circles,
stalking each other,
hunting, hunting, feeding
on themselves, on
each other, no one
gains, no one loses,
save one's own sense,
one's own sensibility.

was it camus talking? one
writes to find a reason
for living—i am
living to find a reason
for writing. and
existence banks on the
ability to exist—the
simple ecology of the
soul. we are all incapable
it seems of living in that
environment we were created
for. we are sea turtles
who don't really like
salt water, or condors
afraid of heights.
          we

hunt ourselves, being
unwilling to live by
other laws of nature.

the word is: to thine
own self be true. and
we lie. the word is out.
the bloody wine changes it.
and the minister says
the words and everybody
bows to them.
          and the
weather hangs over
us all in a poor season.
not even able to live
with the weather! no
ease, no flow of life,
no song in the words, no
song in the wine, no
song in the body. the
poem does not exist, the
poem, does not *work!*
          we
swim in the garish salt
sinking, we climb on
our mates for sustenance,
we support ourselves in
an alien atmosphere, using
every handgrip there is,
and we do not fly.

the blood flows thru
our veins, and the wine
thru our mouths, and
the words thru our
heads, our muddled heads.
give us this day our
daily word.
      and let the
bloody wine leave it alone.
let it grow on its own,
let it flower in its own air,
let it have body. let the
word grow, and be a sustenance
to us, now, and in the hour
of need, let it sustain us.

In the Beginning

i have few clothes and
many books, you bring
few clothes and many
books, still, have no
doubt of it, the one
closet won't be enough,
and tho in our world
there is always room
for one more book
somehow the clothes
will be a problem. tho
in bed there is no
ending the combinations
there will not be room
in one closet for two
suits four dresses two
raincoats two winter coats
and your new spring topper—
if they still call them
that—and the shoes, my
god the shoes, what in
hell to do with all of
them, not even a plastic
shoe bag hanging on the
door of the closet—we
will move to a bigger
place, two closets, lugging
the books and the bed.

The Brushes

a tenacious man
he hung on, he
hung on, that
is, his fingers
clung to what he
had to cling to.

if he had not, what
could he have clung
to in order to sit
around all that
time. that is, the
involvement necessarily
that which life is
made up of, either
you hang on, or your
fingers loosen, you
drop off, because
it's no longer worth
hanging on to it, what
you were clinging
to, that would be.

did you understand
that? while your
fingers were tightening
around? the bones
of them stretching
themselves clinging
to? as to a rock
in the middle of

the ocean? in a
great painting by
watts, hope sits
on a rock in the
middle of the raging
ocean, desperately
fingering her harp.

a tenacious man, and
clung to what was necessary
to cling to, tho fingers
tightened tight as bone
can tighten, tho the
flesh between the knuckles
wore away, tho the knuckles
themselves, showed bare as bones
to the sunlight beating down, on
the rock in the middle
of the ocean, clung to it.

he was a tenacious man.

Aquarius

in february the
water runs slow
under ice
            carrying
the spring, cold
and clear the
weather starts
its turn around.

aquarius strides
sky, water buckets
in hand, he will
pour them, the
land comes awake.

fruitful one,
builder, creator
spirit. an old
man, wise now
he has learned.
it is water we
need. water.
all other things
die or can be done
without.
            water
makes life. and
the ram, the bull,
the twins, the
lion, the virgin, the
archer and the goat

need it, the fish and
the crab live in it,
the scorpion in his
dry desert needs little,
but needs some, and
the scales are
useless without a
man to use them.
            pour
it out old man, make
spring for us, make
life, make the poem
spring, and the
painting, turn the
dipper deep so the
water plash down,
we will run naked
in it, great rills
of water bucketing
down our bodies,
the warm air just
around the corner,
the love blooming
in us—or else
carry us in your
buckets, given
breath, given life,
carried to godhood,
old man at the
beaches of heaven,
old man scooping

the sky for our
sustenance, our poem.

Poem on the Death of WCW 3/4/63

now you are dead
no more to see
flowers or women,
no more great
mullen in jersey
salt flats, now
you are bones that
three-legged
dog can worry, now
you have eternity to
consider those mysteries
your life was
built on, now, if
like marc antony you
too are listening in
heaven, you are even
permitted to laugh
at all of us working
in your woodpile, where
you knew enough to
settle anyone

      —and yet, you
      were always a loudmouth, did
      it have to be so silent, and
      you who all of us knew
      the waste of news, how does it
      happen i hear of your death in
      the middle of music and

and yet i know what men
are saying and what men

will say, and i know
what the burying will be like—
but what of the river above
the falls, and what of great
mullen and the city itself,
what will they have to say?
when we know that yesterday
was supposed to be sunny and
warm, and suddenly it was
gray and raining—what
to make of that besides the
usual inanities about death?

old man you will be
missed! old man
you will be missed!
you will be missed by
children not even made
yet, ears not even
thought of by any young
man walking the paterson
streets—and there
you are, with only
asphodel as you said it
would have to be—oh, christ, yes!
death comes to every man
and we are supposed to be
happy it came silently, it
came after long sickness, it
came while you still could
write a poem; and happy

it waited seventy-nine years—
well, that's just not
much to settle for, old man, and
i think of the poems still
coming, couldn't talk,
could hardly make the
typewriter work, and the
poems still came—

thank you old man
        for all you have
        given, and thank
        you old man for
        all you made yourself

Old Story

a man was out walking his
totem one day and
got lost
          but *the*
map is not the
territory he kept
screaming. neither
was the territory. and
tho he invented fire and
bent his opposable thumbs and
laughed and constructed
memory, he sat there alone with
this big goddamned bear next
him.

          when the woman found
her way to that neighborhood
she was in all her trappings,
her nine little breasts bare, the
three little titties,
the three big boobs, and
the three leathery dugs,
and on one side of her
back the spinning wheel her
uncle had made her, and on
her left arm the leather
gauntlet for the bow over her
shoulder. tho some of her
arms were reaching out
others were pushing away, but
she had never seen fire

before, so she sat down.
it was also unclear to her
as to which was the bear.
soon this was discovered and
she turned into a reasonable
34 or 36, b or c cup. he
took one of her arrows, chopped
it in half, added a six-foot
long straight piece of locust
in the middle, and found himself
comforted able to stand up
holding this while she
slept. the bear kept growling
much of the time, as if to
say: hey bo, let's get
out of here.
　　　　one day she
came upon agriculture.
the bear kept growling,
and every day the man laughed
with the bear, tousled its
hide, and turned back to
her. she still had all
those different arms, but
he thought there was a
key to that too, as to
the breasts. when the
crop of grain started coming
in he said to her: i
think i'll sit down and
invent whiskey. the bear

kept growling.
                next, for
want of anything better to
do, they made a house.
he said, later, it was
to keep the bear out. he
figured he could stand
or sleep in the doorway,
holding the long arrow.

some say that that
first night in the house,
all her arms except two
disappeared, tho those
two kept all the
designs of the others.
in any event, she
said, now you're dealing
with reality. when
you invent whiskey, this
time, or peyotl, for i
forget which end of the
territory we're at, it'll
be religion, and good for you.

he put down the long
arrow and took her
to bed, where they lay
happily for a while, in
all conceivable positions.
then he invented writing.

A Grace

bless this house
and all who dwell
safe within its
living hell

For Matthew, Dead

8 august 1967

at four, it seems to me, he
fell off the stump by the
mess hall, bruising the
hell out of his forehead
and nose, and a good deal
of screaming went on.

how shall we scream now,
when at twenty, he slipped
on a wet, moss-covered
ledge of north percy peak
and fell one hundred yards to
his death. at least this
made that decision for him:
he will neither serve in
lyndon's army, nor go to
jail, nor go to canada.
he was trying to scale the
peak by the west trail.

one half hour ago my own
son at eight months fell,
tripping in his walker.
it will not appear on the
book page of *the times*,
and we laughed instead of
screaming, to soothe him
down. this one has almost
eighteen years to make
his choice, and every day
a peril. good christ,

there are easier ways to
have decisions made. twenty
is no good time to die.

For William Carlos Williams

i am angry because
there are still
birthdays
      and yet they
tell me you
are bad off. that
you are dying
      that
the last time you
went off they
thought you
were gone
      (at the
same time they
say you are furiously
jealous—
      that someone
else can still
use a
right hand!

they tell me you
are an old man

they say when
you write new
verse they will not
take the
last one until
you write
the next

           they are
afraid you
will decide it
is all you
have to say.

it is
difficult to
talk about

: how much land
you moved
into
           it is an old
story
no one is much
interested
           especially
in the face of it
that you are
still at
it.

the inheritance
will not be written
down and cannot be
contested

which is why there
is a need to
say something to

you. said straight
out without the
dignity of
image even—
          since if
you are dying then
you do not need
images now. rather
we should save
things to put
next to you which
you loved and
needed

that it should be
a good trip
          that you should
still be able to
move as it
was

(old man i
am living on
that land, developing
it, i.e., raising
houses and
cutting the timber

—like a dutiful
son the father
hates

—and it
makes me ashamed
sitting here
      no
matter how
busily

The Sum Total

the estimates of my
age varied from nine to
almost dead. the little
girl said nine was a
teenager, teenagers
couldn't have children.
the other kid's older
brother said i must be
twenty-two; then
the discussion veered
to religion, mainly
who made babies. my
son soaked it all in,
learning in the gutter.
the catholic beat down
the pragmatist; she insisted
god in heaven made babies,
while he opted for
men and women. in the end, he
weakened, allowing as how
the mother and god made
the baby together, she
down here, he up in heaven.
the questioning began then:
your mother and father
married? my boy insisted
no! then they aren't your
father and mother she
told him. the other
boy's father had a sword and
three guns, he said—how

many your father got?
this was the only time my
son weakened, he turned to
me as i sat on the bench in
the sun, looking the question
at me. none of them saw
my one finger raised to
him in answer. one, he
said. the other boy backed
off. then the little
catholic girl said that
god was in heaven. up
there, the older boy said.
he pointed. that cloud isn't
heaven, my boy said. no,
said the little catholic girl,
that cloud is air—but
do you know who the first
president was? of america?
yes. richard nixon. no,
she screamed, it was
george washington, and
lincoln was . . .as she
paused i prayed she'd
be wrong. the sixteenth!
i'm four and a half,
my son said, in the
march sunlight, 1971.

The Only Anarchist General

the architecture fell into
place only at night, the paths
led somewhere, the lights
lit them, even the low
wall had a reason finally,
it comforted me walking.

my wife questioned my
orders as if i weren't a
general. the bridge still
frightens me, *not* the ravine,
which is why is it necessary
to make friends with trolls,
constantly. still, i met my people
halfway home, and walked back in company.

my wife questions my orders as if i
were not the only self-taught happy
genius of my household. i note
crests and rises, point out
defensible positions. the
armies move and swell, the
battle is coming. my wife
questions my orders. i am an
anarchist general shouting orders in a
strictly formed landscape. my children
did leave me here knocking on wood,
i walk the bridge alone in the night's
landscape, thinking of low
walls, covering the terrain.

Zen You

as we were involved in this
dart game where nobody seemed
able to hit the bull's-eye which
was necessary to end it, i
turned to my partner and said if
i use zen, that is to say, if i
worry only about the dart and
allow the dart the problem of
the target, perhaps?

      good
christ, no! he shouted—worry about
the fucking bull's eye and let the
dart take care of itself, for
christ's sake.

      i took aim, carefully.
the dart flew straight to the bull's-eye.
oh well, this is the west, we
do things differently, i suppose.

Moratorium

wednesday, 15 october 1969

the little boy wasn't three yet,
and as the crowd grew, carrying
candles, it was hard to know what
he thought about it. he, himself
wasn't carrying a candle but had
a large corrugated cardboard whale,
it had giant teeth, and he held it
high and proud. four people looked
at it and said noah the whale, and
one oohed moby dick, but most didn't
say a thing. it was a silent march.
the little boy got tired, but he would
keep walking, so he gave the whale to
his father. now it rode high above
the crowd; people were asking what
is it? and, why carry a whale in
a peace march?
            i tried to answer
that they were dying more quickly than
us, so it seemed to make sense. some
looked a the two of us very strangely,
a few heard what we were saying.
        they
are killing the whales so fast that
the fleets come back half-full ahead
of time—and a male blue whale can
swim his whole life without ever
finding a mate. this should tell us
what sort of a beast we are, how we've
learned to draw leviathan forth from

the sea, and kill him. from the
beginning we knew how to kill ourselves.

FROM

The Woman Poems

1975

The Lover

every time
the same way
wondering when
this when that.
if you were a
plum tree. if you
were a peach
tree.

This poem, written c. 1954, had previously appeared in *The Dutiful Son*, 1956.

Every Time Wondering

it is twenty years almost since
i wrote that poem, nothing
has changed, every time wondering.
i have changed, the cells in
my body twice over, almost
through a third, the object of
my devotion also changed, the
ways of love also, even those
sometimes subtler sometimes more
brutal having discovered both those
things in myself to a far greater
extent than you dreamed of. that
was mean who have dreamed more than me.
what i meant to say was i never
had a plan for that much as my
head demanded it and it is the only
unplanned venture of my life.
your cunt pants beneath me, above me,
next to me in bed or board, i do not
know what to do with it except approach.
i have no plan of action but myself.
if you were a plum tree. if you were
a peach tree. the line has changed,
even the images perhaps. perhaps now
i would ask for azaleas or exotic
tangerines. what has not changed is
the, or, the *not*, knowing where or
how in this matter painfully i move,
but move. if you were a tree which
had no plan but constantly to reach
the sun, constantly to hold off the

wind, constantly to flower and bear.
constantly to gnarl a little with
that constant fight, constantly
to show a sheen that shows you live.
this is the matter of it, what's
the matter. this is what we talk of.

Gettin' There

twenty years ago i
knew about love. now
i am tired. i study
primary needs.
i wonder about cowboys
going to sleep on
stony ground, their
saddles their pillows,
the hard day behind them.

they twist and stretch
finding the curves they
will fit to, they fall
to sleep gently because
they are tired. the
way i am tired it is hard
to go to sleep, because
i have not been working,
i have been fighting.

gunfighters also go to
sleep hard, because they
are not cowboys. i was
referring to the working
stiff, the man earning
his bread. i was not
referring to the quick
dazzle of sunlight on
polished barrel, the
challenge, the long
drawn out stare, the

tension. goddamnit i
was not referring
to shots fired in
streets in front of
saloons, or tables
turned over.
       like any
old gunfighter i
dream of the ranch,
working together,
going to sleep in
a bed as rocky as
the ground because that
is where we have learned
to sleep. but tired. i
dream of being tired
enough to sleep gently
and deep and not dream
hard enough to remember.

what terrible visions does
she have in her sleep,
my dale evans, who used
to work that bar in
dazzling sequins, and
also slept uneasily, and
is tired of it.

       we dream of
the sunset as the time to
lie down, we dream of banked

fires to be raked
in the morning not
night. we dream of
such hard labors without
tension that the
days of tension without
hard labors will
someday fade into the
sunset. then i
will know about love.

The Lady of Madness

i did not know what
madness truly was until
i heard the truth. she
spoke without lying calling
things by true names.
it was madness.
she said, you were the
ugliest thing i had
ever seen—i was
fascinated.

      i understood
that word as with a
snake. i had never
dreamed another would
say this. i thought it was
my thought, and
lovers, therapists had all
disabused me of my own
notion. i thought i
was beautiful.

      she sat
in my living room and
with her crazy honesty
told me the truth. the
ugliest man she ever saw.
she was fascinated.
by her madness and
watched her body freeze
and thaw. she was mad.

Moving Out

because i was afraid
i hid from her. i turned
my face away so i
could not see her, i
covered my eyes.
i was more afraid
not looking than looking.
i turned to stone.
so i uncovered my eyes,
i turned not toward her
but not away, i saw her
always from the corners
of the eye, i did not
turn to stone, i moved
slowly, but i moved.
oh holy mothers save
me from your sister,
she sits always in the
corners of my eyes,
but i will not turn
away, i will not hide
my eyes. if she turns me
to stone i will stand
not moving, but i will not
turn myself to stone.
if she strips me bare i
will be naked, but i will
survive. if she
strips the flesh from
my bones with her teeth
my bones will stand as

monument to her and to my
stand. if she bites me
in pieces, i will be in a heap
at her feet, at the center
of the cave. for i will
enter that cave if i
slip in my walking, but
i cannot stop walking,
i cannot stand at the
center. holy mother
of life, holy mother
of death, protect me,
i go to join the dancing
mother and i may slip
into the teeth in the
center of the cave.
this is the extent of
my understanding, stripped
bare, that i must keep
walking to find the
holy mother who sings
me songs, this is why
my lifeline continues,
why my fate line is
muddled, who shall
know which mother
protect me, which
guides my feet. i am
afraid of the mother
who bites, i move toward
the mother who dances,

or stand suspended
between them. this
is the hanged man
who was the fool, who
would be the magician.
over all great mother
sits while i whirl in
my head, it was pushing
that head that i almost
turned to stone, i
will not hide my eyes, without seeing
is more fear, without
seeing is no direction,
it is better to see the teeth
eating you, see the skin
disappear, see the
bones turn to stone,
than hiding your eyes
while it happens. it
will happen if it
will. holy mothers
protect me as I walk on.

Screaming Poem

the woman inside me
does not murmur she
screams. it has
been so ever since
i gave up breast for
bottle, the geometry
of shapes for the
algebra of numbers.
this woman claws at
my innards, sits
patiently waiting, beats
in my head, wakes up
when i sleep, occasionally
relents, opening herself
before me. i don't
know what to do when
that happens, draw back,
look for the solace of
straight lines, draw
plans all night on my
checkered graph paper,
plan out the rational life
of a man, and make no
room for magics. i am
torn by the ravening
screams echoing over
and over. love. love. love.

Dream Poem

girl of my
dreams i love
you.
            you keep
appearing in
the street, walking
by me, coming
up to me talking,
even sitting at
the other end of
the bar. in my
dreams you appear
naked or half
so, sometimes your
pubic hair is
wet, glistening, i
do not know what
with, you rub
against me, you
wear my wife's face and
body, you wear faces
and bodies i have
never seen, sometimes
i come in your mouth,
at your face, more often
i fuck you, sometimes
i am frozen, i cannot
approach you, i
am afraid. what
else is new?

Breast Poem

holy mother now i
understand your nine
breasts, now i see
them over and over in
dreams, now i understand
the great sow, the nipples
erected feeding us all.
what i mean is they
move me, they draw
me—mother in this
season of the year your
daughters disturb me.

they run at me down bleecker
street, they walk slowly
across the campus, they
pass by windows where
i sit watching. their
breasts bobble and
bounce, i see them through
thin fabrics and thick,
i imagine them when i
cannot see them, i
dream of them at night.
sometimes they cover
themselves as they
near me, hiding their
breast with their
arms and coats—whether
looking or not looking, seen
or unseen, either way

i am unhappy, either
way i am unsatisfied, the
breasts dance before me,
your daughters disturb me,
holy mother i am forty—
three years in this world,
what do you want of me, what
do you tell me?
           am i
hungry enough for your
taste, do i lust enough
for your body, will you
ever release me? will
your breasts ever dance
before me, will your
milk and your touch ever
fill me, will i
ever be able to dance
before them also?

Monosyllable Poem

holy mother she was
sitting on the couch
reading the paper.
a simple act. in
her short nightgown
her legs open at
the knees, feet
soled, so that i saw
her, the naked
underbelly. i am
speaking of the
fur, the whole sex
hidden. nathaniel
named it baby hole, i
the poet fall back
lamely on cunt and snatch
pussy and twat. holy mother
in farmer and henley's
dictionary of slang and
its analogues there are
eight and one half pages of
small type to say what
i am trying to say and
that was victorian
england. under its heading
of monosyllable whitman
said bath of birth, donne
said best-worst part,
herrick the bower of
bliss, sterne the
covered way, rochester

the crown of sense but
also bull's-eye and
best in christendom,
chaucer the nether eye
or lips, burns the
regulator, jonson, socket,
and the americans, a
monkey. there are also
south pole and spit
fire, oyster, oven
orchard, country down,
cut-and-come again,
niche-cock, receipt of
custom, privy paradise,
scuttle, seal and sear,
standing room for one,
sugar basin, thatched
house, upright wink…
holy mother we are so
afraid that there are no
words. she was sitting
legs open and i saw the
warm fur and wanted
into it holy mother—
as the spanish say
of it it is the
madre soledad, lonely
mother. i wanted into it.

Traveling Poem

you know that we
come to paths
we must take that
do not allow
for going back.
the crossroad
disappears once
we cross it.
in such ways we
approach nearer
or go further
away from you,
from ourselves.
the decision
must always be
made, there is
no standing still.
we crucify ourselves
on crossroads,
on your four forms.
we believe we
are going the
right way, we
do not know it
for certain. at
times we fall
into the teeth,
we turn to stone,
crumbled at your
feet. we move on.

Mother Prayer

for nico dobbs

this child, this
child, this child, this
child. mother you
have love enough do
we. this child.
we do not hear him.
unplug our ears.
we do not see him.
open our eyes.
mother make the
touch come back to our
fingers that we may
feel him. mother
mother mother this
child is talking.
we do not listen.
mother you have
love enough do we.

Lost Son Poem

my son the terrors i did not
describe to you because i
did not think it necessary
have come to haunt us both.
they are not easily laughed
at or learned from but
what else shall we do?
does the moon fall off the
edge of the sky, does
the sun sink? all bears
are not pooh, either,
but it is hard to know
whether the real or the
dreamed are more fearsome.
if you live through reality
the chances are good you
will make it, while the
terrors fade. peace.

Father Poem

i have fathered
four sons, they surround
me in an age of
women, they will
have to fight like
hell to find the
action, i have laid
something very heavy
on their heads. the
youngest, perhaps,
will survive into
the new world.
            myself,
like always and always,
i will be defeated, they
will carry me ball-less and
regal into the house of
the dead where I will
pay for this sin, having
fathered only sons,
having brought no young
women into this world.
but this is in me rock-
like, to do the wrong
thing, to pick the
wrong time. it is
obduracy, pride, a
need to go the wrong way.
yet they are strong.
it is the first time
i have seen them all

together.
          i await
my golden throne,
defeated, regal, honored.
when i get there i
will have a drink and
let them do the fighting.
the fathers of daughters
cannot say this.

Discovery Poem

lady, sister, lover, mother,
woman, i have called and
called my whole life for
your presence, asking only
that you visit. i have promised
faithfulness, i have written
as you tell me. they are only
words. when will you
live with me, be more or
less than inspiration? i
want to know those most
secret parts of you, and
let the poems go damn.
I want to fuck you as
li po tried and died.
I take my chances. would
you have it any other way?
you answer only prayers,
and this is proper. i
can give no more prayers,
and this proper. i
want to fuck you, and
if poems still come
then that will be alright,
but that is secondary.
i have discovered what
is secondary, what is first.

Muse Poem

now she has shown
up at your house,
shares your bed, sits
on your shoulder late at
night. you write
poem after poem for her,
she is back. she wraps
her legs around you,
she holds you tight,
time and time again
you enter that soft
cunt. she will not
stay. at this very
moment, man, she is
here also, fucking me,
showing her tits in
the late summer morning
sun, visiting me in
my bed also. this
is how she is,
man, she shares herself
as she wants it, and
we snatch and
grab it while
she borrows love
and goes. all she
cares about is we
keep lusting, keep
writing the poems for
her. she does not
wonder about anything

except how hard it is
and how long it is
and how strong it is.
it is our cocks she
wants, the sustained
orgasm of our poems.
so long as we
understand this, we
can have her, and
she will visit my house,
your house, any house
there is that hard-on.
if that hard-on
is good, she returns.

we come down to
performance, despite all
we hope for. only now we
know what the stakes
are, we know exactly
what this mother asks for,
and if we do not
deliver, shame on us.
she will leave us.
that hurts, even
when you learn how
to handle it, even when
you tell yourself
you do not care. we
care, mother, we care.

which is why we ask
constantly for your body
not your mind. we
want to sink ourselves
in you as deeply as
the water, we want
you around us like
snow or the dirt of
the grave,
          we light
candles to you, mother,
we sing songs, we
even puff our chests
out, show our feathers.
finally we learn
to write songs
for ourselves.

which is when she returns.
and if we have learned
she hangs around some
more. she is a whore.
what else did you expect
from the holy mother
we sing to? what
else could she be and
be faithful to
herself? what else
could we love, and
be faithful to her?
what else could our

hearts break for?
why else would we sing?

Mirror Poem

women i love and
watch these days walking
around mirrors bits of
glass in their sleeves,
their shoulders, set
glinting in light and
sunlight, in dark
corners of bars, medusa
i think of, the
stone mother only
approached through the
safety of mirrors to
look on her with
open eye straight you
turned to stone, stone
mother did this, stone
mother i know, why
are these women wearing
mirrors bits of
glass in their
sleeves set on their
handsome rounded
shoulders, to keep
my eye glancing
off? to distract
me? to lure me
on? that is
unlikely. they
are mirrors, mirrors
keep you from real
objects, objects are

real but not in
mirrors, your
hand slides over
the surface, quicksilver
was what they used
to make mirrors
from in alchemy.

as if in a stone
set polished in your
belly or your
touch i was to see
the world, when i
ought to be looking
direct. your belly
button straight into
where you live. no
stone. no mirror.

is this the totem
of their being?
mirrors? stones?
i tremble as i
walk, as i look in
dark corners of
the bar, light
corners of the house.

how came this
mother to my life?
how came medusa? i

tremble as i walk and
look. it was her
sister. it was
her sister. i wanted
her sister. i thought
her sister was here
beside me. i will
fall, turned to
stone, and cannot
move. the mirrors
are my signal who
she is, always. if
it was only my
wife alone, i would
not worry, would
consider it fashion.

it is so many women
i look at these days,
mirrors flash and
blind me, stop
me cold as stone.

Season Poem I

the season is changing.
every three months
it does so. three moons
with each mother is
the allotment. ecstasy
held us all summer, and
death comes now in the
autumn. next we will
hide from the tooth
mother here cold winds
swirling round her head
and no matter how we
hide she will find us.

spring mother, good mother
bring us the light.
ecstasy mother i
swear to you if
you take me and hold
me next summer, i will
make it worthwhile.

the song of the braggart
man, yet how else
holy mother to have me?

Definition Poem

the goddess is
mother daughter
sister wife with
or without
man. each act
is separate and
contained. the
man does not know
any of them. he
clutches each
portion as his
own. what
does she care?
it is as if each
act performs itself.
she does not care.
he will suck her
tit for milk, he
will caress her
breast for love,
he will tweak her
nipple for sex,
he will draw away
in fear from
touching of her
magic. when she
is young and growing
she says where
do i put these?

Prayer Poem

holy mother of the
perfect tits. holy
mother of the not
perfect tits. holy
mother of the body
which asks. holy
mother of the body
which denies. holy
mother whose arms
reach out to take
me, whose arms lash
out and deny me, whose
cunt opens, warm and
wet, whose cunt lies
folded tight in its
hair and its lips,
holy mother of all
the mysteries hear
this, stay with me.

in the end and in
the beginning stay
with me. there is no
end holy mother that
is not beginning.

stay with me.
holy mother though you
leave you are here.
holy mother when you
are here i am

alone. holy mother
you have nothing
to do with this.
holy mother i build
you out of my
own head and this
is my disservice.
holy mother i
have not trained
myself other, except
in secret moments
when i discover
the perfections and
imperfections of your
breasts, cunt, ass,
arms, et cetera.
in such holy moments
i have found you
again and again.
in the end
is the beginning.
do not leave me.

do not let me fail
in believing. holy
mother come to
me or wait as
you are i will
move. i will touch
you and hold you.
i will see you

at last. do
not leave me at
this moment as
you have left me
at others. do not
let me leave you
now as i have left
you before. let
me look at you
and touch you.
holy mother i
beseech you. holy
mother i pray.

holy mother of
the perfections and
imperfections let
me open your cunt
or give me whatever
strength i need
that i may leave.

in such leaving to
find you or make
you find me, holy
mother, because i
am hung at the middle
of the square and
the circle, i go
neither right nor
left, up nor down.

this is the service
of no one, this
will destroy us all.
give me the strength to
stay or to leave
holy mother.
give me the strength.

you sit silent
so that i have
only my own voice.
this is the answer
to prayers, the
end is the beginning,
the leaving the coming,
the perfection the
not perfect in all things.
mother gives and
mother takes away.

First Poem for my Last Son

for six months
he babbled in tongues
now he speaks american

which is what you do
you filter out all
the sounds you don't use

meanwhile i take lessons
with the master and he instructs me
to walk like a baby when he learns
the groin relaxed and the weight
carried below the navel

how much will i have to learn
from you oh my best beloved
while my culture falls on your head
and exactly who will win as
i go down and you come struggling up

the race is of course to the swiftest
yet gravity is on my side at last
and you have only strength
and your babble is too light-hearted
to last
        you will engrave your
head and body with loads too big
and your weight also will move upward
into your chest and your air will turn bad
there is nothing else i can tell you

but even when you were
speaking in tongues i didn't listen
and I never know even now
when you are telling me something
and this time for me
there will be no next time
no new sons to not hear

i have lost it again
as with all my sons

but i will try to learn to walk
at least while you can teach me
but you must bear with me
since it is hard even though
i try my damnedest
         while your feet
find their own ways to friend
to mother brother father
going to the wall for support
relaxing the groin and carrying
the weight below your navel
while keeping your legs fluid
and the air in your around you good.

E. P. 1885–1972

for a long while you
were owned by everyone,
an object, an
enemy, someone to
defend or excoriate;
owned but not sold
you said come my
songs we will sing
of perfections we
will get ourselves
hated; you said every
day as the sun rises
make it new; you even
said a long time ago
we elect either knaves
or eunuchs to lead us;
you were talking of
america; you were
not a nice man; you
taught us all the
language and you
reinvented the forms;
you lived these last
years in silence, telling
us something more; you
walked naked all your
life putting your
life on the line for
the taking, you were
bought, owned, now
you are dead and in

the perfect way of
this world, now
only the poets can
own you, barter
your brilliance in
their lonely rooms.
parlay your winnings,
fight over your
coat you never once
turned, now the
world is done with
you and only
the poets own you.

A Letter To Philip

can i any longer address you dear phil
when i have spent the morning
ordering my life in unrealities

the rent the food the clothing
the ten percent allowed for luxuries
the baseball register and the sporting news

which things are necessary in my world i say

i have written my oldest son
and sent a check to celebrate his nineteenth year
and i have yelled at my youngest son
to celebrate his curiosity which stalled my writing checks

my head is awhirl with money and games and family
and you are in the real world finally

now you are not only my brother
but the world's brother and the ant's brother
god's brother and even the foolish writer's brother

which is why i wonder how i dare start a letter dear phil
wanting to know the honorific when you must recognize none such
but there is a need to honor you somehow
as you honor me by every step you take

i think of you sitting silent sitting speaking walking
and i am honored
            i have been given this grace to know a decent man

who does right things while i whirl in unrealities
writing checks and poems

A Poem for the New Year
31 december 1973

i shower carefully, scrubbing
my body, preparing myself
for new year. having been
a dirty young man shall
i now start being clean?
i watched your body while
you dressed. 'desire springs
in me yet, i ought to be
satisfied' is a line i wrote
fifteen years ago. now we
have grown older in our ways
and in our heads also. now
i dream of medusa, where it
was always her sister who
presented herself. now medusa
strangles me, and i am saved
by the old poet, he helps me
break loose. he tells me
he's never yet seen one would
hold on if you fought long enough.
i hope he's right. i woke from
that dream stiff-necked and
sore from the struggle, but
i had lasted another year
from the freezing of my breath.
today i saw a basilisk in my
dream who also tried to freeze me.
i woke abruptly, thrashing, safe
again, as he scuttled across the floor.

the basilisk does not grow
older, does not ever change.

we walk on, and sleep each night.
he said: hold on, hold on,
until the new vision comes.
it comes, it opens up,
is always comes. but some years
are long waits in which we
sleep and dream of basilisks
and mother medusa waiting
waiting to stop us. we cannot
stop. we cannot stop her.
someday we will welcome her.
medusa stay way from my door.
let me look once again at
a woman's body without the
mothers intervening, getting
in the way. let desire rise
in me still, i will be satisfied.

mothers: under the running water,
in this dirt of my life,
in the cold air of new year,
in the fire which sustains
and consumes us, bring me
to the next new year,
to the next growing old,
to the net growing up,
to the next growing out.

If There Was Sense

to get there you would
have to come up the
missouri into the white,
or coming from the
west, cross the badlands.
from the south the
sand hills would
block you, you would
have to work to get
there. i sit here
writing, thinking
of where i should be
if there was sense,
thinking of all the
provisional brigades
silent, unmoving,
wondering where they
are, where we are.
thinking of the land
lost, the country
lost, the power lost
because no one moves.

if there were sense the
brigades would be forming,
the long columns would
stream toward wounded
knee. if there were
sense the passes would
clog with us, the
prairies would shake

with us, long files
would come riding up
from the south
carrying the deserts with them.
          quakers
ready to lie down,
abolitionists risen
and fierce, lord
grizzly and the
mountain men, the
woodstock kids,
the angels even,
king's people, malcom's
black moslems, hanufi,
jews, irish, italians,
chinese, even the
buckleys screaming
for freedom. great
columns of smoke on
the horizon by day,
great plumes of dust
rising, great pillars
of fire by night. this
is a picture i could see
if there were sense.

if there were sense
i could hear
a gigantic shout: give
it to them, whatever
they want. give it

back. give it back.
let them have it, they
can do no worse. a
great irrational shout:
give them south dakota,
give them the black hills
and the great plains,
the prairies, taos,
blue lake, the mountains,
the father of rivers, the
woodlands, give them
manhattan, long island,
terre haute, the high land.
give them the thousand
lakes and the thousand
islands, give them
okefenokee and the great
dismal swamp, give them
their land. they can do
no worse. give them their
hostages against fate, their
lives against death, give them
give them give them give them.

Serving Notice

i will not be
that single daddy
my friend had
roasting a leg of lamb
every sunday
slicing neat slices
through the week

these kids
will eat differently
every night

their clothes will fit
and not be put up with

and they will wear
their hats and rubbers

and in my bed
i'll dream whatever dreams
are necessary

and i'll curl those bodies
i can or want to
around my body

and i'll take the necessary time
and i will not make
leg of lamb each sunday
slicing slices through the week

Celebrating the Peace
9–15 may 1975

if you celebrate the end
of a war you are celebrating
that war.
                go home my
townspeople into your own houses
that is where peace begins.
                        the war is starting
what speeches will you make
or hear that have not been
made or heard by you before?
                        the war is starting again
in what way by gathering
to reconstruct air that was before?
how by gamboling before the orators
on sunny days to make a peace?
                        the war never ended
you are gloating your are waving
flags in triumph.
                no god no master
the flags said in paterson so
long ago the silk strike the
only flag i wish to see no
wars no governments no states
they take umbrage like a human being.
                        the war goes on forever
forget the dead people, forget
limbs piled in earlier bloody
wars, forget blasted innards, eyes
seared, leaves gone, earth scorched—

yes we did that too—forget
homeless people, peopleless houses,
forget helicopters falling in the water,
forget the gold that weighs those choppers down.

                          the war is over but a ship has been
                          captured by them and retaken by us
                          and the choppers have landed the marines
no rhetoric will make it as it was.
the nature of peace changes by the war before.
dead grandparents would not recognize this peace.
and theirs would not recognize the peace they knew.
so many wars.

                  there is no peace
if you must celebrate it, parade parade
march your banners and your selves you
are victors you have triumphed over
other people you have won. what? you
have won what? peace is the absence
of a triumph it is quiet singing in
your house and bed it is turning to
your own concerns and pleasures.

                          there is heavy small arms opposition
                          the enemy has released their captives
stop celebrating. *celeber:* frequented
or populous. wars. occasions of wars.
they are frequented, populous, the
people stream one way or the other
under orders or because of fear. peace
comes from *pactum*, a bargain, a bargain
made that we shall be left alone.

                          several choppers were downed in the assault

                              the ship has been returned
                              the men are safe
                              the marines are still engaged
let us lay down this burden down by
the riverside, let us feel peace
in our hearts and minds let us have
no more celebrations that celebrate
what we have beaten lest we forget
what it was was won and we become
conquerors and strut as certainly
as jack boots in another place.
                              the fighting goes on
                              the war goes on
crow triumph. peace cannot ever win.
destroy the world to save it. we
have heard that before.
            there is no peace
build such a chain of people
you will not need to celebrate
you will not need these gatherings
except for the work of hands. these
other works will destroy us every time.
do not go to the party. do not
celebrate the end of war you
celebrate the war
                              there is never any peace
                              there will never be peace
                              the war goes on
                              the marines are landing
                              we don't take shit from anyone
                              we'll show them

125

peace is not victory but a natural state
do not celebrate the end of war
nobody wins

AT FIFTY: A POEM

1980

I

necessarily
the goddess is
unattainable
     nympholepsy
       that rapture attained
       straining for the
       unattainable
and the stroking
touches only surface

yet is causes her
to rise near those surfaces
the evidence is in
the sounds

XII

a fool is always a fool
for young women
            when
young a young fool

now a middle-aged and
soon to be an old one

before they had
to be crazy and young
now they need be young only

and where before
they said it was because
i was a poet
            now it's because
they have this hang-up see
about older men

XIV

at last i understand
the young
        are for
the young
you will never warm
these bones with
that flesh
        that flesh
will warm bones
that need no warming

oh you will come
because i need never
because you want

also i will watch
as he watches
you and see his
face light as
mine stays dark

at last i
understand this

VI

seven-thirty in the morning
couple in shiny english boots
whipcord jodhpurs riding caps
blue broadcloth shirts whips
walking down hudson there
and no stables that way

VIII

they set up headquarters
registered the prospectors
declared the site closed
to any others
vaccinated the colony
against yellow fever and meningitis
banned women and alcohol
announced that anyone
firing a weapon
would be expelled
set up a loudspeaker
to play country music
during off hours
and the national anthem
at morning and evening
flag raising and lowering

each night soft-core
pornographic films
are shown on the airstrip

XII

eleven years ago
i stopped making love
to watch cleon jones
put the team ahead
in a crucial game

stopped the act of love
to watch baseball
on television
a ballclub in
a pennant race

not important except
to remember committing
this act life vs art
art vs culture vs
the individual whatever

eleven years later
there is always something
embarrassing to remember
something we did that was
shameful ridiculous and
shameful something
to wish undone

but that marriage is gone
and the team won the pennant

I

bewildered in the
morning heat
i take an apricot
i take a plum

though they taste
good to me only
the first bite
is accurate in
what we expect

finally they cloy
too much or not
enough of what
we eternally desire

nothing is ever
perfect in this world

one bite is perfect
still it leads
to another

V

the topic sentence says
by any rational calculation
the potential benefits
vastly outweigh potential costs

the first major point is
suppose one or more
great oil spills blight the region

it is answered that
the economic loss would be great
but not greater than the losses
from the eruption of mt st helens
or the droughts that strike
the grain belt every decade or two

the second major point is
the ecological damage
would also be terrible

it is answered that it would not be
more terrible than the damage
inflicted on the deserts of the southwest
by poor land-use planning

the third major point states that
those who prefer to go slow
note that the oil would not disappear
if it were left in place for another decade

and this is answered that

unfortunately the timing of the flow
could be critical to economic stability

so in summing up it says
every effort would be made
to exploit the alaskan oil reserve
with minimal environmental damage
but whatever the valid hesitations
they should not be allowed
to cloud our economic future

to which the teacher comments that the
rhyme interjected into the last
clause of allowed and cloud is
distracting and unfortunate
and that our economic future has
been clouded anyway since the
industrial revolution began
since man began
to eat himself

FROM

GENERATIONS

1983

Child

not to be able
to touch one's
mother not her
arm to lift her
what she did to
cut off touching
now not able
to lift her while
my brother does
he learned how to
touch from her
i did not

What My Father Said

about words with unpronounced letters in them
silent like the "p" in swimming

how to go fishing with a can of peas and a baseball bat
open the can and sprinkle on the water
when the fish come up to take a pea
hit them over the head with the baseball bat

don't ask for too much
i have tried to get brown sauce on my meat for twenty years

if you are going into a partnership make sure you hate him
you will keep an eye on him all the time

if you want to be a garbage man
make sure you are the best garbage man there is

don't sleep with women of the street
that are dirty

the apple didn't fall far from the tree

Mother

i saw her sex
naked, pouched
grim as her lips
sunken her
teeth gone

her one eye
glazed open
her lost eye
sunken shut

her sex naked
barely haired
apparent

the nurse
businesslike
while i oh god
seeing it

naked and hairless

The Oldest

mother
was stone

teeth bit

sisters none
i longed

two wives
no longer

never daughters

now on
i flower

loving him
same mystery

we share that

Ritual

this shawl, son,
this wrap, this
fringed garment
is your sign

you have come
of age
        you may
read the words
and live by them

you may approach
the book and read

you may carry
the words with you
as you in this shawl

it is of the desert
and it has covered us
everywhere
        we start
from nothing, from
the dry dust
        we grow
with the word
until we flower

flower well

Life

i wish
there were rules
to give you

there used to be

my father gave them
to me even if
they didn't work

he lectured
day after day
how to behave
what to hope for
what to wear
what not to do

but those rules
have all gone now
and I no longer
know anything

still i will have
to find something
to let you sleep
each night out there

it's a hard road
you will need
some rules to last

i wish too
i could say
i love you
some other way
than just the words
but the words
will have to do
since we can't
hug any more
the same way
now that
you've grown big
but i hug you
anyway
with these words

and add
i'll have dinner
on the table
when you get back
tonight from
your first day
at work
        out there

Statement to the Citizens

we are here, working,
hungering for bread.

you are there, living,
hungering.

      can there not
be commerce between us

A Village Poem

in the summer of '73
i'd had twenty years
in this place
              my own
history

              a history
of places, things,
a piling up said one
a night-mare we
are trying to escape
said another

i sat in the white horse
with my son, nineteen,
beside me
              the last time
we sat together in a bar
he was five, and the bar
was the cedar tavern
and a man gave him
and his brother each
a dollar for a toy

what history had done
to the white horse was
to turn it too small
misshapen dingy dark
ceiling too close
not even memories

me only forty-three

i started to be cynical
i started to be sorry
i had brought him
i started to apologize

but i caught a look
in his eyes and i saw
he saw the ghosts
saw he saw dylan in
one corner, behan
in another, saw he saw
all writers everywhere
saw those drinking
their lives away
still writing their
words saw the white horse
was bright and real
for him
          i shut up

and i remembered
my own history then
remembered the walks
twenty years ago
edna st vincent millay's
house or maxwell bodenheim
seen on the street
cummings in the back
of the eighth street

jackson pollock tackling
the eiffel tower in front
of the albert hotel
and all the bright moments

it's today for someone
else right now walking
in here young and eyes open
seeing the brightness

it's never, not
this particular way
for someone not here

it doesn't matter if
the crooked streets
the little houses and stores
or history or art
keep bringing them here

listen, some want to work
and will do so, even

      franz kline sat in the cedar tavern new hat on head
                      bought at cavanaugh's
   he always dressed beautiful
         pollock walked in talked drank got angry
  grabbed that hat threw it on the floor jumped on it
             threw it

ledge on top of the bar too far to reach

franz bought a round
            a week later
pollock appeared again bought round sat talked stood up
pirouetted said
look at my new raincoat just got at brooks brothers
                franz said it is
beautiful
            jackson bought more drinks sat drank got mad
jumped up ran
outside ripped off coat stomped it in gutter threw into
road under a cab
and came in
                franz bought another round

it is history whether we
want it or not
it is what we learn from
it is where the paintings
come from and the poems

what? melville different, or
dreiser, poe, well yes maybe
james different but not
even that different

all young people come to find
a place and themselves
and their history and
to make their history
and to make their connection
the whole long line

of crazy people working
at work finding right places
where work is possible
where friends are possible
the whole long line yes
shakespeare had a place
villon peire vidal ovid
even homer singing
in some bar then

not that to drink
is to create or that
to be crazy either
not that to have friends
who do is to create
not even that to have
a place is to create
and certainly not that
this place is the only place
but that this place exists
and it might as well be
and we keep coming here
and using it for that
it is our place where we are
and it is the place where
the work gets done
as even tonight it gets done
and tomorrow when we are alone

because we have this place
and we believe in it

and it is still bright
and perfectly formed
and it is where we are

Lessons I

the war was over
        they found helen in
deiphobus' house

        he had taken her
there after paris was killed
        against her
will

        she had given herself to paris
willingly enough

        deiphobus was
not what she had bargained for
                so they burst
into the house
        both menelaus and
odysseus
        to kill these two

                but as
graves tell us
        "some say helen herself plunged
a dagger into deiphobus' back"

this and the sight of her naked breasts so
weakened menelaus in his resolve
that "she must die!" he threw away his sword
and led her in safety back to the ships

Lessons II

the point isn't
that he fought that war
or vowed that she must die

it isn't even that
they left together
spent the exile in egypt
went home to sparta
together

      it is that
moment
      and the dreams
that led him to it

the dreams
when someone
leaves us for
another

      and when
she is beautiful
in our eyes and
the other's and
the world's eyes too

so he raised his kinsmen
and their armies
and he fought
to kill her
and avenge his honor

the sight of
her naked breasts
ended this war

all through that war
he must have had
this certain dream
every little once in a while

this dream in which
he finds himself
again and again

he is bringing gifts
—beware a greek
bringing gifts—
yet bringing gifts
to her
            to ask
forgiveness
            since
we do decide we are
the one who's wrong

we ask forgiveness
in those dreams
while wide awake
we know how
wronged we are

in those dreams
we beg acceptance
and a smile

oh yes we know
that we have wronged

why else be alone

so alone we hope
to be forgiven
having done that wrong

in this certain dream
helen sits waiting

we open the gift
for her
            it
astounds her
and she smiles
then laughs

we too smile and laugh
as she accepts it
thus accepting us

so good in the dream
we wake sick with anger
having dreamed it

real anger that
somewhere deep
we still suck around
still beg

       even
menelaus begs
for helen's
naked breasts her
smile and all

even when we know
the loss and time
gone
       know that
it's over
       dead

we want it that way
and we would not
change it
       still
we want love just
as it used to be

we want buttermilk
breasts that perfect
face that acceptance

the tender love
she had once felt

for us we thought

even knowing all this time
she deserves her paris
and he her
          perfect for
each other
          just as we
had thought we were perfect
once
          even for the world
they are the perfect
couple coupled

yet we ask why
yet we dream why
yet we cry why
paris why him why
her
          where did i
go wrong

Acts

my son and i
walk out
in this cold october morning
toward his school

we hold hands

his other hand
holds a pennywhistle

he will use it
to accompany the guitar
in the morning singing circle

at each corner we cross
i am looking for you
while he and i walk and talk

i keep thinking
we will meet
at one of those corners
our paths intersecting
just as the clear note
of the pennywhistle
occasionally crosses
a particular chord
of the guitar
in the structure of some song

i keep thinking
in other words

that there must be a point
that we cross in common

and so this morning
we do meet
and walk together
half a block

he and i still
holding hands
you next to me
on the other side

one small moment
for you and me
to register our selves

and then later
after he is in school
and you are gone
i drink my morning coffee
and read the paper
again intersecting
this time with the world

i read that hugo zacchini
the first human cannonball
is dead

i read that all his life
he wanted to be a painter

and that after his retirement
he taught art to young kids

'yes, say for me'
he is quoted
'that my cannon
does me much honor
but do not
forget to add
that it is as a painter
that it is my ambition
to be known—

day by day
my cannon cannot give me
the thrills
that i can get
with my brush.'

lucky man who
day by day
first in malta
then throughout europe
then in the old garden

before me
a little boy
holding my father's hand

went one hundred and fifty feet
reaching an arc of seventy-five

where was my father headed
what intersection
was i going toward then

a flash
a puff of smoke
a roar
and he would go
hurtling through the air
in an idea
he conceived
serving with the artillery
in world war one

so i hurtle toward you
and toward this poem
aiming for some corner
of our lives
where we can meet
this morning

i do not know
whether or not
there is a net
it never occurs to me
to wonder about it

the flash smoke and roar
take the forms of
an alarm clock
and the radio

and a small child
needing his bottom wiped

oh this act also
will be carried on
by my son
just as his son
learned to enter
the mouth of the cannon

oh i also wanted
to do something else

oh i also learned my methods
in some previous wars

A Beginning

we are here
in this place

we hunt these
new beasts

we take their
hides and their furs
to the island
to meet the ships

we were brought
to do this
           in this
new place where
fog covers all
too often

the sun tells us
how the year moves

when the sun rose
in the notch
the priest prepared
for its coming
it was the new year

now it is darker
it is four months later
we watch the sun
dying slowly now

it will die
faster and faster
and the dark will come

we will be alone
in this new place
without the ships
for the winter

building our piles
of furs and hides

we were brought here
for this
          the mother
came with us
her belly filled
by the father

                * * *

there are others here
with different faces

i have taken one
of their women
and they have taken me

we show each other
what we do

they know
these strange beasts
but i know the mother
and the father
and the coming
of the new year
and they
do not

her skin is a
different color
and the paint
on her face is
different too
and her hair springs
alive under my hand
and is black

i gave myself
to her
        my friend
gave himself back
to the mother

that has never
happened before

he asked the men
on the ships
to take him home
from this fog

they would not

i asked him
to take my woman's
sister
           he could not

he gave himself
back to the mother

he could not eat
the strange things
that grow here

and the bear
of this place
was different
to him
           he was afraid

i saw that this bear
was our bear's brother
and i welcomed him
and he welcomed me

and i eat
the strange things
that my woman
knows how to cook

* * *

ah, even the rocks
are different here

still we can build
places to pray

and the mother of mothers
mother of heroes
the father of fathers
who is the sun
of the new year
all have travelled
here with us
in the ships
over the water
and the priests
have come
with the prayers

and we make
our homes here
and there will be
small ones too

to grow big
in this place

where we meet the
ships with our cargo

Cities This City

the things they always complain of
coming from outside and again on leaving
there are so many of us crowded in here
and we are all so aloof and alone

we here are always alone
every city alone in this country
which has never learned to accept its cities
every city on its own alone and doomed
born to lose written on it walls

yet here we stay in it and keep coming to it
we keep pouring ourselves in and out
we light the skies with ourselves sometimes
sometime someone may be watching those lights

we are using ourselves people bodies
instead of trees and grass and earth
we eat people instead of eating the land
we watch love and hate bloom all around us
not weeds or flowers as in so many other places

we keep thinking we are making something
from our own bones and blood and flesh
and not like the others living off the land

we know that the oldest city was so
we know that the newest city will be so
it will always be the place the others use
while they keep complaining about it
while they send what they make from the earth

while they send what they can't use
while they send what they want to sell
for what we have to give them in return

they send their poets and their whores
their painters their conmen their dancers
their thieves their dreamers their murderers
and we add our own to these yes

maybe you cannot have one without the other
maybe indeed you need all in this city

i don't know if this is right
i only know the need to use one's self
to bet on one's self even when it's fixed
rather than watching things grow outside one
and then killing them and then piling them up

and when the ports and the crossroads
and the easy jumps across rivers
aren't needed any more for their commerce
the songs and the poems and the dancers
and the drawings of things imagined and real
which come out of the rub of people against people
will keep pouring out of the city's people
feeding the people who are angry feeding them

this feeding started in the first gathering
and will go on to the last gathering
because while the world build itself in the void
people alone hunger for each other always

for whatever it is that only people can make
for whatever it is that only people can feed each other

Cacti

I

love comes
once a month
these days

i am not complaining

it drops on me
unexpectedly
just as rain does
on cactus
in nature
in the desert

it floods me
for a moment
forces new growth
drains away then
in sandy dirt

i am planted
in sandy dirt
insecurely

it is all
a conceit
of course

still
i am not complaining

i am stating
facts of my life
at this moment
and perhaps
from now on

i am
after all
still alive

i have survived
a long time

and i have watched
all the flowering plants
of my life
wither and die
because i did not
handle them
properly
or water them
as they needed
or perhaps
if the new thinking
is correct
did not know
how to talk to them

i am not complaining

i am learning now

that the cactuses
the succulents
even my crown of thorns
continue to grow
to survive
to flourish
without love
or water
more than once
every month

and it has taken
all this time
to learn this
and to learn
that they are my plants
as my life

yet it is true
the kangaroo vine
she left here
is still going

its tendrils reach
out to the lamp
down to the radiator
but this is an aberration
the exception
proving the rule

II

it is
opuntia rufida
the blind prickly pear
that first declared itself
as if in acknowledgment
of my own blindness

it has refused to die
despite the fact
that i expected it to
and perhaps even
out of that expectation
encouraged it to

nevertheless
every time
i left this house
for any length of time
it sent out
new shoots

so that
when i returned
it had children
to greet me

they jutted out
and curved upward

at odd angles
and at odd junctures
from the main body

they were
bright green
even though
rufida itself
tends to blue
to gray green

now this cactus
will even grow
while i am home
and the shoots
continue to be
phallic in nature
just as i myself
have fathered
nothing but sons

cattle relish feeding
on the joints
of opuntia rufida
in the wild
and on its
small fleshy
bright red fruit
which i have never seen
but the plant
is supplied

with glochids
or thin barbed bristles
which fill the areoles
where spines would grow
in other cacti

these glochids
readily penetrate the eye
and blind the cattle
feeding there

next to rufida
there are two cacti
grafted together
as one

at the top
gymnocalycium
asterias
a bright orange globe
with tuberculate ribs

each tubercle swelling
just below the areole
so that the cactus
is called chinned

under it
cereus ocamponis
of which it is said
old stems turn

dull bluish-green
and the rib margins
become brown and horny

mine fits this description
it must be very old

the book also says
gymnocalycium
is self-sterile
in most species
and that hybrids abound
in this genus

next to that pot
on my table
a different variety
of cereus stands

it has just
been given to me
and i do not
understand it yet

it is tall
it is light green
it is shooting
a new growth
straight up
from its top

we watch each other
carefully
we will have to learn
to live with each other

behind this front rank
stand the others

to the left
echinocereus
a hedgehog cactus

it is self-contained
and silent too
as are all cacti
but has attracted

from somewhere
an unnamed succulent
which has sprung up
beside it

the succulent
is very young
but already tall
with small thick leaves

it is ready
for its own pot
but i am afraid
to transplant it

it is not
related to
the jade or
happiness tree
as they call it
in england
which grows
separate and distinct
in its own pot
a handspan away

this succulent
i am told
should have its
leaves wiped clean
every fortnight
but i do not believe
this happens
in nature

new york city
is not nature
and we do
the best we can
in its grime

since it and i
continue to flourish
i credit such happiness
as we have
to this jade

doing its best
in this house

i told you
i am not complaining

at the rear
of all these plants
rearing proudly
is euphorbia
my crown of thorns
which i rescued
from friends who
despaired of it
tired perhaps
of its stance
or its obduracy

having watched
the cacti grow well
i was emboldened
to try this one also
and brought it home
even though then
i did not know
its name

i was born
in east virginny
to caroline
where i did go

and there i spied
a fair young maiden
her name and age
i did not know
says the song

this plant
grows tall
with thin green leaves
small sharp thorns
and a woody curving stem
still it is
a succulent
i am told
and it has
a rare
hard
and terrifying beauty
that makes us equal
as we face each other

III

these plants
enlarge my landscape
and make it green

no this green
is not leafy
or flowering

it is not
the beauty
many depend on
but it does not
leave me
and it gives hope

spikes
spines
thorns
thin barbed bristles
protect it

and when you touch
we hold on

we do not
grab you

you must
come to us

like the rain
once a month
out of nowhere
out of blue
and beautiful
skies that rain
otherwise
on leafy
flowering plants

this is why
i am not complaining

i am learning
how to live

i am learning
i am neither rose
nor weed of the field
but did not know that
and suffered long
trying to be such
trying to grow that way

i am not complaining
i thrive
even though
i grow older

i grow stronger

the only ones
that i hurt
these days
are the ones
who do not understand
and try to
grab me
or come to eat
too ravenously
and are blinded for it

or those
who laugh
to see my
brown and horny
rib margins
my colors of
blue or gray green
and cannot accept
that this
is beauty also
and a way
to keep living
in a hostile
climate
in a soil
that would not
support an ordinary beauty

those who cannot accept
another way
to live

Houses

eighteen years ago
i left your house

it was your house

yes i brought home
the money
       we
did it that way
in those days

now again
i am showering
in your house
        "her bath, which she takes
        because he wills it so.…
        in his tub. in his water. wife."
        was even more years ago

        i do remember
        and i don't

getting undressed
i saw a silk robe
hanging behind the door

and the jars of oils
the soaps and powders
lining the shelves
beside the door

all in neat order
beautiful things

things beautiful
by themselves

and things beautiful
on your body

i thought how all
that i have loved
all that i have missed
is in this house

don't misunderstand me
i am not speaking
of romance
or rekindled love
or even second chances

nor is it a new obsession
with neatness
from one who's always
been the other way

if anything it might be
a lesson for younger lovers

perhaps even
for the ones
i come here

to see married

our first son
and his beloved
as if that action
by our child
allows you
to invite me
and me to accept
and that is why
i am in this house
far from my own

far from that house
i have learned
my own lessons
in building

in any event
a lesson
here also

      in first love there are things
      we grow to as a habit
      and will never be happy
      without again
            sexual appetites
      change
            it is easy
      to grow cramped and leave

still i say again
no matter what reason
for the ending
            there are things
we grow to as a habit
without which
we will not be happy
so it is
that years ago
i learned to love
your ways
so clean and neat

ways that cared
for beauty
and were beauty
and were
without
compulsion

            they happened

around me
without my knowing
and they were
caring ways

i've smiled at times
these eighteen years
realizing that
the only reason

i have folded up
my washcloth
in my bathroom
is because
you wanted it
that way
instead of crumpled
                    while
all that is remembered
of our sex
are bits and pieces
of some short-lived scenes

no touches
no movements
underneath me

a few sighs
or groans
a few importunings
one to the other

a picture of your breast
or thigh or face or hand

but i remember
very well
the house
you gave me
and see it
here again

perhaps this is why
i am so pleased
that i have changed
to see it
through the eighteen years
for what it is
and what is was
for me
       not that
you have not changed
it's clear you have
it's clear we both have
but his part of you
has not
       and the part of me
that sees it has

***

now it is after the shower
and i have changed
in a much simpler sense

i am in some
new-found finery
a fop or dude
inside my western shirt
my shiny boots
and all the rest
as you have never seen me
and i feel i fit

in your house now
a stranger perhaps
because i am so proper
where as your lover
i stuck out
                it is
the proper way to visit
i am saying

but on your shelf
among the oils
and powders
is the frog
i bought you
our first christmas
twenty-five or more
years ago

i see it now

made of brass
a candleholder
on his back

            i knew
you wanted it
i saved the five
or seven dollars
that it cost
            i'm glad
to see it now

it means
you really wanted it
it wasn't just a fancy

you kept it with you
and you use it now

there is a stub
of candle in it

perhaps some nights
you bathe yourself
by candlelight
          i
see you that way

long baths as
i remember
          while
i lay in bed
reading
          or wrote
that first book

the one with poems
about you bathing

or just waited
in our bed for you

the waiting was not

always good
               it
destroyed the marriage
i have sometimes
thought
               but not
the waiting
while you bathed

that was part
of what you gave me
as i lay in bed
and dreamed
               a sense
of preparation and
of love and care

it was the other waiting
caused perhaps by what
i did to you or
what you thought i did

then after a while
i could wait no longer
and i went
               you
were just as happy
and that pain
is gone now

i remember only
there was a woman
of rare beauty
          a wife
who bathed herself
so slowly in my tub
that i wrote poems
about it
          in that first home
i ever had
          a home you gave
to me long years ago

***

before the shower
i had taken a nap
in the guest room
of your house
          i
dreamed of us
of course

we were naked
but only from our waists
on down
          as   if to say
this is where we are
right now
          with the sex
outside and open

we were so afraid
in those days
and we didn't know it

in the dream
our tops were covered
our brains under cover
covered prettily
to face the world
and each other

perhaps that
might have worked
if we had known it then
to cover up our brains
and let our sex hang out

but we didn't know it
and we kept on talking

so i woke from that nap
this afternoon in your house
at peace with the dream
despite its sexual content
which aroused me
        it was
not you so much as
talking to myself
the good doctors
tell us that

at peace i went into
the bathroom for my shower
where i found my past

and was at peace
with that too
as i am now in my house
writing this to you

the house i've fought
my way through to get to

this house which is
not so clean and neat
as yours
            i am a man
i need a woman's touch
might be the pity of it
but i've learned to build
without it
            but now can see
how pleasant such things are
and where they come from
in me
            that is what
i did not know
            and what
i now do know
and will remember

Preface

there has been a welter of talk about the function of art, its meaning, its value, and, indeed, its relevance. the talk has gone on for ages. just the other night i heard an artist—a sculptor, but the discipline makes no difference—say that the most important "meaning" of his work is that which the viewer bring to the work.

i recoiled in horror. one hears this refrain over and over again: the professor of poetry who says that only the sound lasts, while the sense changes; the critics, who, these days a least, seem intent on proving a case for themselves at the expense of the work under hand, and therefore insist that there is no meaning beyond the language itself; the audience which has been educated to believe that "it means whatever i want it to mean"; the artist him or herself who responds by saying "it doesn't matter what i wanted it to mean, as long as you respond somehow."

i meant for these poems to mean things. i had things to say in them. i hope they say those things to you. i don't mind if they say other things to you, or make it possible for you to say other things; both those responses are legitimate as well as time-hallowed. but i damn sure hope i've written these poems in such a way that you can "believe" them; if i say it is snowing, or i am looking at a desirable woman, or it is hard to face breakfast without any teeth, you will understand them at the level at least and move on from there.

every poem we remember has to do with real things, no matter how far the poet's imagination or invention takes it from those real things. we remember the poems because we have had responses triggered in us by the poet's perception or those real things, as well as by his imagination and invention. every poem, is an investigation of the world we live in, the way we live, and the way we treat ourselves and others.

i hope also that the poems allow you to play as they have allowed me to play—with language, with ideas, with juxtapositions, with life, because human beings play, and that play makes living possible. perceptions of the universe are play, must be play, and there are no better examples than poems or any form of art.

that is the meaning of these poems, generally. the specific cases can be understood, always, on that level. the language exists to help communicate those investigations one to the other. whether the material communicated is important is not important, because time and people will winnow out the "unimportant." but the things themselves, in fact, whether love or hate, war or peace, are always important. we are drawn to these investigations, and we learn from them. if we handle them badly, we produce bad poems and those are forgotten—or "unimportant"—or, perhaps, just meaningless.

i hope that these poems, mean something to you. not each poem to each reader, but one or some to each. if they do act in that way i have succeeded as a poet—and as a human being, and the poems will be "important."

The Teacher

battered by sensibilities
i pretend the poem is easy

but it is not easy not for
me not for you ever at all

i give you simple rules
and if you follow them
the poem is simple

i give me complex rules and
again the poem is simple
because the complexities
are as bad themselves as
any of my sensibilities
and they writhe and intertwine
until all i am left with
is the blank landscape the
simple landscape the landscape
covered with cliché alone

you all pay attention to
my simple profundities
and do not understand the
simplest fact which is
that despite its simplicity
the poem is a difficult thing
and we are prey to all
its various vagaries and
vagrancies and shifts of
time and space and meaning

battered by sensibilities
in front of the class i
take deep breaths pretending
the poem is easy to write
and you write simple poems
and i praise you for them
and wish i could reach as
simple a conclusion as
i pretend is there before us

it is but still the sensibilities
batter me and batter the poem
and the poem winds on itself
and becomes complex no matter
how simply i conceive it

and becomes simple no matter
how profoundly i reach for it
in the midst of its complexities

if you want bread love a baker
says the old folk wisdom and
that is simplicity enough and
even perhaps sensible also

The Garden

i have taken
to buying flowers

i had inherited
three vases
        memories
from my childhood

one slender brass
one chinese a
touch of class
one forties awful
decorated glass
with glassier flower
buds stick on

i fill them weekly
with a few bucks worth
and i have begun
to see them
        irises
made for watercolor
or watercolor for them
peonies so lush
they fill the room
opening and fading

daisies last

sweet william
has too many

variations

                    i
grow confused by them

statice stands
tulips bend
lilacs die too soon

these are city-bred
conclusions as i know

but they are conclusions
in a world made new

where flowers never were

Spring

this letter
is long overdue

it is late in spring
and it was promised
in february

it is on the second
of that month
that persephone
begins her journey
up to earth

the letter is not
for her but for
her lover dis who
as lawrence tells us
sends that spring
chasing at her heels

she flees his dark house
and he sends flowers
snapping at her heels

friends glorying in
spring in the country
mistake me also

as we mistake dis
and send letters
to tell each glimmering

change of season
as if it did not happen here

so the letter is
to say we know it here
as well
        that spring
comes just as surely
every time it should

i announce spring
in the city

flowers on bethune street
and on bank
        in little
plots of earth exposed
around the trees that
stalk the sidewalks

snowdrops first as usual
then croci now tulips
daffodils and where space
is wider cherry trees

others have pictured
this place differently
they feel sorry for us
locked
        but dis knows
cities too
        the flowers
come snapping at her heels
even here

so i announce spring

Anarchists

alexander berkman
shot the wealthy mr frick
because mr frick had closed
his steel plant in pittsburgh
and had gone home saying
the strikers had bad manners
and he would not tolerate that
and he would hire nicer people
and he sent in the pinkertons
to kill the strikers

well the truth is we live
in a place which considers this
the shooting of a rich man
an atrocity while the murder
of poor men is at best sad
and not even really considered
a crime at all *n'est-ce pas*

because after all mr frick
must have been nice or
he wouldn't have been rich
and as for alexander berkman
if he was so smart why wasn't
he rich is what we folks ask

and the rich get richer while
the poor can afford only dying
day after day after day after day

FROM

NEW HAMPSHIRE JOURNAL

1994

Chaos

CHAOS is where
we come from

FORM we reach
occasionally
then fall back
into chaos
to start again
renewed

INCHOATE
means beginning

comes from the root
TO HARNESS

getting into harness
is just the beginning

how we plow and
what we plant
determines the field

the field
determines
what feeds us
while we wait
to fall back
to grow again

In New Hampshire

the earth moved
this morning

we were asleep
curled in each other

the building
trembled around us
and we woke

we trembled with it
in sleep and out

the brain asked
is the building
falling down

but that deep memory
in us all
knew it was
the earth moving
and we on it
moving with it

and the fear
held us fast

we trembled with it

Country Alba

every morning
we sit over coffee
eyes to the window
looking to find
birds feeding

they do not come

filled and waiting
the feeder hangs

friends say
it takes time

i know birds feed
for other poets

words soar
about their pages
darting pecking

i change the water
beckoning them
every other day

and she waits
to fill the feeder
through it's not empty
it hangs untouched

the birds
do not come

no words soar
peck about
these pages

Gryllidae Achene

city poets grow used
to roaches sharing
their words with them
so gryllidae achene oh
common house cricket
when you catch my eye
you startle me just
as the roaches i'm
so familiar with

i can't adjust to this
notion that here in
the country we have
crickets in place of
ubiquitous roaches

the black presence
scuttling across my floor
is so similar it
alarms me equally

yet i know crickets
bring good luck to houses

in fact i have gone looking
for the little houses
the chinese make of bamboo
to find one for you
to live in to keep you
content and here with us

and besides there is
a difference of course
gryllidae achene you
sing in the dark while
the roaches merely scurry
away from the light

and where your name
comes from the french word
for clicking and creaking
the roach is reduced
from the spanish cucaracha
and where cucaracha comes from
i have not yet ascertained

well what does it all mean?
do the french have nicer
if noisier houses while
the spanish casas are
dark and food-filled so
they attract the
indestructible roach
or does it mean the french
eat up all their crumbs or
does it mean this house
is luckier than the one
we've left behind
                and
will you oh cricket
oh gryllidae achene
be able to survive as well

as the roach which survives
everything even they tell me

the bomba atomica or will you
and your luck run out
with us while la cucaracha
inherits the earth

A New Hampshire Journal

for kyle landrey

alone in bed
i hear a
chipmunk or squirrel
inside the walls

he smells the remains
of this day's food

he is trapped behind
the vent turning and turning

he cannot get out

surrounded by snow
i cannot get out

we shall spend time together .

         * * *

the snow fell

the radio gave weather
just seventeen miles away

sunny and clear it said

the snow still fell

later it was indeed

sunny and clear here
and i had bought
my new boots by now
and with them on
sat talking looking out
at four men on the roof
shoveling scraping hacking
banging ice with hammers
to break it free
and save the roof

at all times one
of the four stands idle
his orange gloved hands
folded on his shovel
leaning in a universal stance
the eternal work ethic

* * *

no birds
animals across
the roof by night
then deer track
morning outside
the door

under the snow
what breathes and lives
waiting out this time
to spring alive

what grows silently
without my knowing

what dies as quietly

* * *

this smallest thing
i can give i give
in my lonely bed

this littlest thing

in my only bed

i give this small thing
it is all i have to give
still i give it

once in a while such
giving is perfect
and even then we doubt
no doubt you suffer now
with such doubts your
belly soon to swell

i would say this
i trust your belly
and your timing

you grow in season
is the point

* * *

i was talking to
someone beautiful as
she was talking
of someone beautiful
and she said this
other stood naked posing
she had learned to model
knew what she was doing
and she the first beautiful
one said on seeing this

she gasped inside asking
are they all this beautiful
if only they relaxed
and knew what they were
doing doing it

struck by this beauty
of the first woman
as she was struck by beauty
i thought and said then
we are all that beautiful

i meant of course just
the two of us that beautiful

but this allows all others

        * * *

a letter from the other coast
says jobs there are no jobs
yet the prices rise and rise

he writes a large number
have been saved through the b-I
and other government largesse
yet notes many people still starve

the numbers of unemployed
do go down since so may
are off the lists they
no longer count as unemployed
but only i suppose as
lumpen or in new terms
the underclass the man writes

and he cannot believe
the beloved ike once said
every gun that is made
every warship launched every
rocket fired signifies
in the final sense a theft
from those who hunger and
are not fed those who are cold
and are not clothed or sheltered

he is furious that president
could know of such priorities
and not care to act on them
or couldn't given political
necessity which cones to
the same cold the same hunger

the economy fails as it
is planned to fail for
the benefit of the few
and those few continue always
to tell us to be happy and
like fools we are happy
and ask for more leaders
more weapons more killing

knowing we shall never see
missiles as lovely as we

* * *

a new typewriter
a sunny afternoon
my birthday
a photograph

frolicking in surf
my own aphrodite

so soft her breasts
she says better than

bo derek and is right

aphrodite in your service
now another year
year after year
to desire and occasionally
reach occasionally know
both love and what
one does is not so bad

might move one on

eternally my aphrodite
rising from the sea
in some far place
the next not yet known
or dreamed of
for the next new year
the next new birthday

* * *

the inn will not accept
any child younger than six

i wonder whether to lie
about my friend's daughter
hovering so near five

my own child plays games
with a new friend

in another city two parents
grieve the loss of a child
just become a man and dead

crushed in snow on a dark road
i have nothing i can say
sorrow cannot be given
or taken away from another

he was good he was bright
he was handsome he is dead

the other children play
or live by rules we put on them

there are no answers
to any of this no reason

oh let them play
in peace and love since
we all must die too soon

* * *

his voice cracks
on the telephone

this is the sound
of real grief
not imagined

i do not know
how to cry is
the first thing

what a price
to pay for this lesson

to learn to cry
at the loss of a son

and in his voice
a thousand miles away

but i would cry with them
tonight if i could

this is what friends
exist for to be with you

we must all learn to cry

* * *

there are no answers
but we are more able
to bear that each time

i cannot tell you more
though you ask

you ask and asking
make me feel wise

we do our work
we believe it matters

if we cannot do this
we will stop working

we will stop

we will stop all

Animals

the young goat
tethered on the far
side of the blacktop
stands on his hindlegs
trying to find more
green leaves on the
young tree from which
he has already stripped
everything within reach

the old black dog
for which his owners
had spent the weekend
of the fourth of july
building a run shaded
at one end and
with a study doghouse
got his rope tangled
in growth at the
shaded end and
spent the hot day
unable to reach
his water

he was ill with
heat stroke when
they returned and
was ministered to
all that evening
but later slipped
free and escaped

no one knows
where or how
just gone

and i whose
body fails me
miserable with
the tumor swelling
pressing against the
cerebellum walk
slowly like an old
man afraid i won't
make it looking
at the goat
the empty doghouse

f

COLLECTED LATER POEMS

1997

For Hoyt Wilhelm

the ball dances in
no steam no smoke no
hook across the plate

thrown properly
you see the seams

it doesn't behave
the way it ought to

the sluggers flail away

the catchers lurch
left and right
up and down

if you do hit it
you've got to
make it move
with your own energy
it has so little
of its own

everybody hates it
managers hitters catchers
announcers even complain
it isn't really pitching

the arm lasts
a long time though

and the ball takes
forever to arrive
and the man keeps
throwing it
and no one ever
times it correctly
except by accident
or chance

and if you keep
on doing it
eventually they let you
keep on doing it
even while they hate it
and you keep on and on

the strong arms get tired
the fast balls lose an inch
the curves start hanging
the sliders don't slide

the constants are
the knuckleball
and the wild swings
and you hoyt out there
for a million years
and the e r a dropping dropping dropping
while the catchers
keep scrambling to stop it

i'm glad you made it

as least one of us guys
with nothing but knucklers
caught their attention

made them say at last
it's the right stuff
even if it does look funny

Poet and newspaper columnist Joel Oppenheimer (1930–1988) grew up in Yonkers, New York, and was educated at Cornell University, the University of Chicago, and Black Mountain College, where he studied with poet Charles Olson.

Oppenheimer published more than a dozen books of poetry in his lifetime and was included in Donald Allen's seminal anthology, *The New American Poetry 1945–1960* (1960). The posthumous *Collected Later Poems of Joel Oppenheimer* was published in 1997.

An avid baseball fan, his nonfiction book documenting the New York Mets difficult 1972 season, *The Wrong Season*, was pubished in 1973. Oppenheimer also authored *Marilyn Lives!* (1981), about Marilyn Monroe.

The first director of the Poetry Project at St. Mark's in-the-Bowery Episcopal Church, he wrote for the *Village Voice* from 1969 to 1984. Many of his columns are gathered in *Drawing from Life: A Selection of Joel Oppenheimer's Work from the Village Voice* (1997). Oppenheimer taught

Photograph: Elaine LaMattina

at the City College of the City University of New York and New England College.

Oppenheimer died of lung cancer at the age of fifty-eight in Henniker, New Hampshire. A selection of his papers is held in the archives at the Thomas J. Dodd Research Center at the University of Connecticut. He is the subject of the biographies *Don't Touch the Poet: The Life and Times of Joel Oppenheimer* (1998), by Lyman Gilmore, and *Remembering Joel Oppenheimer* (2005), by Robert Bertholf.

Acknowledgments

These acknowledgments do not comprehensively acknowledge all of the appearances of the poems in periodicals, newspapers, chapbooks, books, and anthologies.

Names and Local Habitations: Selected Early Poems 1951–1972. Winston-Salem, North Carolina: The Jargon Society, Inc., 1988.

The Woman Poems. Indianapolis, Indiana: The Bobbs-Merrill Company, Inc., 1975.

Names, Dates and Places. Laurenberg, North Carolina: Saint Andrews Press, 1978.

At Fifty: A Poem. Newton, Massachusetts: Arts End Books, 1980.

Generations. Buffalo, New York: Bob's Slow Foods Editions, 1983.

New Spaces: Poems 1975–1983. Santa Barbara, California: Black Sparrow Press, 1985.

Why Not. Rochester, New York: Press of the Good Mountain, 1985; Fredonia, New York, White Pine Press, 1987.

New Hampshire Journal. Perry Township, Wisconsin: Perishable Press, 1994.

*Collected Later Poems of Joel Oppenheimer.*Buffalo, New York: The Poetry/Rare Books Collection, University at Buffalo, 1997.